SLINGSHOT

SLINGSHOT

CYRÉE
JARELLE
JOHNSON

Nightboat Books   New York

Copyright © 2019 Cyrée Jarelle Johnson
All rights reserved
Printed in the United States

ISBN: 978-1-64362-009-1

Cover Design by Saxton Randolph
Design and typesetting by HR Hegnauer
Text set in Perpetua and MaaxDisplay

Cataloging-in-publication data is available from the Library of Congress

Nightboat Books
New York
www.nightboat.org

CONTENTS

false sonnet embroidered w/ four loko empties

Wishbone/Fishbone asleep on my wing chair
central to this scene's rent glamour
       until the body replaces her. The seat bare
       for I, thick thighed human sitter who nurtures

a contempt for the subway. Slick benches
vice my abundant meat. Signs chastise
us *smaller, smaller* as though we were finches
— shit, some of us are.   Yoga Pants is surprised

       at my public comfort, unearned in her eyes.
       Wobbly and painful her interruption
into my lap, both her legs across mine.
Pure nuisance. No ask yet all intrusion.

I unfold my form against her fluster.
Rage pelts hate. I fire polished stones
hardened from ichor IV drip. Clustered fists
mute as rubber bullets. I'm a full grown

       whatever-the-fuck, and I will devour any
attempt to subdue me   with monstrous animality.

SLINGSHOT

pastoral w/ well water kool-aid

Brook breaks into pooled black
        ink & boiled shale dirt.
        Ominous petrichor
            dares our heroes to shirk
their higher ground for beads

off dappled white oak leaves.
        Drained from endless drownings.
        After flaying blizzards;
            before forsythia
and his jaundice treaty.

Back then she thought yellow
        was enough to please her
        so she, cruel, pinched the jewel
            the honeysuckle's hull
cerbericaly guarded.

Her nearest neighbor shared
        a shack with his children
        his wife's belly of stones.
            She offered thirdhand clothes
& no news. Arms stretched long —

she knows what's contagious
        and close enough to spread.
        If the ceiling's maw yawns
            wide enough for deluge
or possum, bandage trash

bags so trouble can't slide
right in. Don't leave one rat
unmurdered. I snap brooms
so quick their neck meat skips
while mama swigs her dreams,

then another vodka.
Then two handles of gin.
Then three boxes of wine.
She's Easy Jesus Christ,
She's The Mother I mourn.

magenta

The kind my homie Leah calls screaming
Vulva, a sparkler through grey
Hair with glint of mercury.
Quickly we become elders in this city
Smears our fingers like new murder.

They're my mentor, with Sinti-Roma's bleeding tarot.
When I was a kid they wrote *Femme Shark Manifesto*. I lived
A childhood with pink books and gem mischief.
That zine is the zine that I mean when I mean *the zine*.
It was a roll call for fem/mestyles,
Pumped a saline shot of sadness,

But at least there was fucking to look forward to.
I wanted to grow up and be them and then be their friend forever
Wash all their dishes
Eat drying pizza out the box
So I filled three bags and moved to Oakland.

It was blank verse for ten months and fucking
I slept on Anna's couch,
As ever, and wrote for weed magazines.
Hot-handed roof gardens blush pink as lips.
The other ocean coughed out boys with limps and lisps,

Prince punctuated all my trysts
I dated a cop for about six months
A future flush with killer gear

He won't tell you about the rapes but paints and sculpts
Them in his face
Where eyebrows once were and should appear.

Alas. This poem can't reinstall the skin
Nor grow his eyebrows back again.
His fetid hide has ceased to be for all of our eternities.
For this, only impotence.
A poem mauve with fizzy goiter
Flaccid as Pacific sick spray spewed

A poem to coil you in fistulae of yarn and stars.

jersey fems in the philly zoo

a flamingo knows,
even without pink lipstick,
fem is a feeling.

black boots. Raritan
tap water memories flow.
murderous brown geese

fly from Johnson Park,
arrive, then turn up their beaks
'fuck dis sposta be?'

they inquire. I
find cover in the leopard
print fem next to me

because here, always
someone's looking, someone's stares
caught in plexiglass

refracting the light
in your life. no. it's not you.
they look to consume.

especially spring,
and when the ice cream melts
before it's lapped up.

Philadelphia
is lilac and lightning strike
before a great storm.

electric strangers
cuff biceps unexpected
back draws straight — horror.

they look to consume.
they desire to control.
predatory birds;

eagles, owls, all.
swooping down with catching claws,
no glass to hide you.

I want my armor
an exoskeleton, tough
hewn of crushed velvet

bristling with defense
a kevlar of tenderness
enveloping me.

this is what happens
when the tree blooms: the axeman
runs to chop it down.

this is what happens
when creatures meant for the deep
somehow crawl ashore:

they will be lapped up
by the hot eyes of the sea
pulled tight by strange hands

knives licking their necks
the scent of wisteria
fireworks: flash/bang.

flash fire, roll flame
clip wings from those who maim us
declaw them all, bare.

maybe they will burn
corralled, while lights dance in sky.
steaming macho ash.

and if they must live
then make me invisible.
hide me. erase me.

harold mouthfucks THE DEVIL

Harold is 52. He drives roundabout 66 miles on I-95 to and from the tube factory
in Branchburg. He punched the glass over the speedometer yesterday. The automobile's

tools of measurement are bloody, but he never checks them anyway. The cupholder
clutches a 3/4s empty can of Budweiser. It's 6:15 in December and the moon is maroon

in the black latex of Pine Barren sky. His backseat is tetris'd with cans of O'Doules.
Nice try, Harold. A white streak darts through the road as if chased. Harold's nausea

pulls the string beneath his tongue, presses its thumbs into his throat. He opens the car
door a little, its leatherette split from heat. It's as though his insides are tearing
as puke punches through him, bilious, no longer containing food or even beer.

He lays on his back in the puddle he made, only an inch too shallow to drown in.
A figure above him. Behold, a goat; its ocular golden cleft. Harold's bleary eyes peer

and correct. The goat stands dripping stygmata and flexing bicep tattoos.
Solve. Coagula. The goat has titties and a dude's face and no genitals to speak of.

The thing no one ever told Harold about THE DEVIL is that when you see them
you get uncontrollably aroused. Sexually. Harold doesn't like any gay shit

he ran off his eldest stepchild at 14, who is me, the narrator. Kicked his face and ribs
until he fled and in her fear the mother called it justice. But here he is, cock stiff before THE DEVIL.

THE DEVIL strides closer to Harold on cloven hooves, in leather assless chaps, unbothered
because they're THE DEVIL. Although THE DEVIL doesn't have a binary gender expression

it's still gay to Harold. THE DEVIL values consent so they ask Harold
if he would like a fellatio and Harold nods and screams *YES! YES!* 6 covens

of genderless magical practitioners arrive for orgies nearby because THE DEVIL is into that. Everyone in the vicinity is on the verge of ecstasy when Harold starts to cry.

THE DEVIL turns the burnt out O'Doules cans into piles of glistering gold coins, and we stimulate ourselves with their ridged edges. Harold snatches his boxcutter from the pocket of his vacant jeans.

He slits his own throat. He's dead and he's gay and he's not sure which is worse.

an elegy for the family (w)rex

> "O Lord, Sula," she cried, "girl, girl, girlgirlgirl."
> —Toni Morrison, *Sula*

Your heel, a shiv slicing open the hide
of some heedless, anonymous creature
      creeping beneath the El's wide lip shimmer,
      circumspect to the stomp of your danger.

Six blocks of rank asphalt & ruined sidewalk
beyond the splintered door jamb you shot out
      screamer, big-talker, inevitable
      drifter. Wind and tight handfuls of glitter

thrusted among Philadelphia's blood
stained Japanese Maples, ridged *Watchtowers*
      — their covers splatter-painted, rain tie-dyed.
      You showed your nipples at my old home club
            ATLANTIS: THE HIDDEN TREASURE, awash
            with resign. What you want, you'll never find.

Just resign. What you want, you'll never find.
Nonprofit motivation, still employed
      (Not in nude halls where once I had hunted,
      but in carpeted cubical devoid

of lucrative potential.) Skeptical
slash resentful of sheltered coworkers.
      I'd hear my call to the stage   *DYNASTY*
      LIKE-NO-OTHER! as I snoozed through meetings
         snorted awake, afraid of defunct fees.

Together we were The Family (W)Rex.
Every night, we staged our plays. Seven days
a week. Your ass went on for forever,
my plush thighs broader still than dinner trays.
The Brocade Sling! The Vintage Ermine Muff!

One silk slingshot, one vintage ermine muff
four limp black wigs: real hair and plastic thread.
You stashed vices in spider holes: codeine
tabs, Xanax, and cash. You gathered toys spread

out on the floor into trash bags. My niece
barely had any before you arrived.
Her uniform spotless, her blankets rags,
a glowering, sullen streak in her eye

for which I don't blame her. A child, scared.
She rages, mopes, and cries until she chokes
opposite Auntcle as novice au pair.
Her mother elsewhere, swathed in Newport smoke
devoured by the slick beast that bore us.
On your leave, at first, I felt empowered.

On your leave, at first, I felt empowered
by my sole successful attempt to set
boundaries. (I'd later have so much to grieve.)
In the moment, I was spiteful. Contempt

tinted my view of you. More than old friends;
at sixteen, we were closer than sisters.
Once we sprinted through Exit 10, Tercel
sputtering towards some strained family scene.

Your gossamer Joyce Leslie dress was lewd
as you bent over the rosewood casket,
to peer into the face. It looked like you.
Zipped up in plastic...that's it as we bumped
Jay-Z. You clipped your hair, served Amber Rose.
Will you stay awake as the illness grows?

Are you falling asleep? Just in repose?
Does your gown bag like white tees in 00s videos?
Does the cocktail leave you gaunt and morose?
Do you know of your fate? Is it sour?

I'm far away, but misting as you breathe.
Around me veins split, perineums tear.
Infants twist inside their cozy pouches.
Comrades shit as they bleed out in bathtubs.

You wane wan, drawn as you blanch in moonlight.
But you've beat the piss out better things
with nerve enough to try you. O sick sage,
I can't protect you from what the lump brings
but I'd've stayed on for the ride and rubbed
your heels as the shiv sliced open your hide.

a machine of mahogany and bronze I

My son as an ugly girl child, eating collards
from the butter tub on his birthday. A party
of he and I and to him I am no one. He was
not the first to think, he is not the most recent.
Imagine him twelve—soup cooling lips wet with pot liquor
fingers sticky from ripping lemon sheet cake
to fistfuls while I am in the other room.
Here I am in the other room: attaching my tracks
with pins, adjusting my girdle, twirling
the telephone cord around my pinky finger
talking to my man, maybe
about something later and nasty.
GO TO BED at the child pretending.
Hear his shuffle grit the peeling linoleum
the answer a slammed door already splinters.
I imagine him asleep. I go to work.
He's old enough now to spend the night alone
I tuck ankle boots with open heels
and open toes into the cheeks of my bag.
Secret spray deodorant. Jean Nate. Nine outfits
in sandwich zips. My beeper. Two money bags.
Handful of garters. Sneakers. I creep
out of my own door ignoring the silver fridge light
a thread through the keyhole, reminding me
he is awake, though he pretends.

*   *

Everytime I see my mother
on that same good mom tip
her bests: she tried her best
she wanted what was best
having chosen the best way
there for the vision. Not

she's on her same bullshit
 always crying and ranking
she did the best she could
she's living her best life
she knew how. As if object
 fraught. Not the worst.

I put my finger up as stop
when I came to pieces under
to powder on my face. Head
all the time tells me how good

no more of you talking at me
your roof, specks of ceiling cracked
board assaulting wall plaster
while I grit my teeth, smelled blood.

I see her face in backwards
time. I am nine again, fifteen
climbing down a fire escape
loud enough for her to hear.

When I see my mother I am
only as old as the rupture.
How trust shrinks when salted
How mouth clap shut at facts.
This is the last last time.

Memory and nothing more
forever better pulled apart.

She tells me what she'll
buy him for his birthday.

*

Folding a slingshot gets easier. After a couple years
your shoulders soften. You find yourself
in universal control of your extremities dangling
from the rod handless. Work endless until
the day is a metaphor for three lines joined
into the circles that measure your arm. Lexus
taught me this trick: the bands of morning day
night. The first time I asked Sage to help
with no words. I called her silently to me
from the best chair in the mirror. A perched raptor
gyrating endlessly—the day one oily shift
noon to three AM. Sleeps three hours, calls
her children awake, rubs snot from their noses
pries sand from the corners of their eyes.
I am the child she swaddled in neon cords
without dropping her Newport long
hair half-curled. She repeats the ritual—
one loose shoulder, the other, the fold/twist/sinch.
A slingshot is exactly what it promises, nothing
more: the commercial jag, sweating in its pouch
flying short and fast, meeting its mark then resheathed.
I tip her as the custom. The time she prayed
with me cost. Her baby's shoes bump
the tin dryer drum. My breasts hung framed
by glow strings as I descended into memory
of her kindness. ceiling drip
        christening my vinyl mattress.

In dreaming this evening
walking through my grandmother's
          rose garden in Savannah, bread
factory down the road, smell of moon soaked
          air, after a spring rain kicks
          up the dust for a minute—everything,
                              a little cleaner.

everything, relaxing into its moist
grooves.
          Mema at the center
          of her garden, wearing green
          gold embroidery at each
          hem   alive in ghostliness.

          She always had a garden
          black with loam, shale
          from the center of the earth

          their yellow arms reach
          higher. Each fluttering eye pink
          as Coney Island cotton candy. Scarlet
          as suede church shoes. Pistons jut
          their tongues like a gossip among
          thorn's filigree.
                    They lean to touch
                    each other, arching their back
          into the grip of her emerald gloves.

          She whistles "How To Reach
          The Masses" singing
          what she remembers.

Sky and its other, shadows
        each to each.
Heaven wide and ancient in her face.

She pinches my cheeks
      then pulls my head in two
      joined halves   a locket of flesh.

*   *

At noon The Organization coalesced at   *   park
     & Freedom Alliance was there
     & the so-called nonprofit leaders were there   for promotional reasons

& Kamilah brought the cardboard coffins   with the names
     of everyone disappeared from   *   Signs alleging *torture, homegrown blacksite*
     inhuman conditions the charges all bundled in her grip

        her daughter clinging to her belt loops   tiny legs almost running
                   to keep our pace.

& the street medics were there with bags of Maalox   lavender essential oils
     calm voices   blue vests with plus sign pockets.

& the press was there   *   most notably,
     forefingers and thumbs in a square   squinting around for a scapegoat
     shoving cameras & boom mic into white faces   shouting *what do YOU think of all this?*
& the press was there   *   most notably
     inferring, spinning, solidifying, referring & just plain lying.

& Kwame didn't show up to be press liaison, so instead of just coordinating, I handled that, too.

& Jordan came through with the chants
     & some had the nerve to be fire —even though I had talked a whole bunch a shit.

so *Assata Taught Me* was there & we had nothing to lose
     but our chains   when the chant hit us we knew
     for sure   all huddled in the warmth of one another.

& *our allies* (who had said they'd buy food for folks)
     brought a big ass pot of raw beans and rice   with a lonely fucking bay leaf

but hunger arrived

                and some drank down the warm intentions.
& the beans rendered themselves more edible the longer they sat

& we were almost   grateful. Others pushed the stiff grains of rice
over the rims and ridges of their mouths until

               the starch   pulp separated from the pellet inside.

Then the cops got there
    first in their unbroken line   of sneering laughter
    their polished riot boots & girthy vans   replicas of themselves within it.
    They spilled from behind their plastic shields all clear plastic tower
            club tentacle   names printed on the front

but the practice of freedom was also there
& we were prepared to hold the line in ritual
I could smell the healers' perfumed smoke behind me.

        The street medics
        talking about fear & grief
        in hushed tones

    we will hold the line as a practice of freedom

& we did as we marched onto the highway
    arms bent together   a machine of mahogany & bronze

& a second flank of cops appeared before us
    in the on ramp
    with a blockade
        but the chant had finally reached
        the back of the line

& our gears cranked as the lever of force was inserted

        struggling to move forward

               against their wall of unbroken windows

                  their unburdened line of blue.

& the street medics knew pepper spray was next

        & the healers knew to tell them

               so important were seers to our collective vision.

Goddamn it, the white dude anarchists are here

        with telescopic batons & cardboard shields

               faces covered to the eyes in bandanas

                  faces pressed into the mug of a mask

                  & I knew that shit was about to go down

                     cuz aint nobody invite these mufuckas.

Yet here they were. Fuckin up immediately.

        Two tall ass white boys faces *V for Vendetta*

               & Yankees jersey charge the cops, box with a handle

                  bashing in front. Yo, we're screwed.

the cops send up pepper spray again; folks scatter toward each other

        old women coughing in the crowd

               & little kids dropping their signs

                  with tears welling in their red eyes.

& when I can see again, someone is holding Alisha

        by her arms, her legs still moving forward

               a gear torn off from the rest of us

                  so we stopped & watched

                  phones sideways in our hands

               knowing we hadn't planned well for this.

this impulsiveness,
            this ungalled entropy.

Vans roll up
horses roll up
cops pour out
vans roll out

helplessness sets
failure announced
press condemns
pundit amends

bail posted up
Lish gets out
we burnt out.

*

When the pigs rolled out
         our team scattered
                  eager
to eat something besides
         whatever climbed
         the high sides
         of that pot.

I knew we should talk about what just happened —
debrief and strategize. I didn't care

         I needed to clear my head.

I texted Asar
         cn i grab lyk
         2 dubs from
         u asap?

         He said meet him at a park where once
         river rats dove for reasons we don't understand.
         I abandoned the powder blue barricades and traffic cones
                  trotting heavy over horse shit

         an army of chemical ants stomping
         across my pupils

         I turned my face towards
         the strengthening rain

         lighting fire to whatever
         the Maalox didn't catch.

Tears falling into my earholes
dripping off the sides of my head.

my hoodie drenched from amethyst
to eggplant, the sleeves sweating
        as I walked into the wind.

        Off the side of the pier
           the green-grey water
              slapped the rickety slats.

The loose ends of Asar's cornrows
blowing frayed over his shoulder,
crisp and oiled as he stares out across the ocean

        tip of his Newport
        glowing orange
        in spite of wind & water

square earring glinting back shine
as the street lights popped on
anticipating sunset

short and skinny as ever
wide feet wrapped in spotless
red and black sneakers.

His eyes velveteen set
among clusters of freckles at caramel
cheeks, looked at me almost squint
as I walked up, smiling small.

He licks his lips out of habit
and turns towards me, blank faced.

We shake hands
          as though we're strangers
                    only now meeting.

He grabs
my hand again
to swap the dubs
for my $40.

I ask if I could bum a short
          or if he'd short me.

          We took two pulls a piece
                    on the sopping bench
                    our backs to the percussive sea song.

Sitting too close together
          to pretend to just be friends
                    too quiet to pretend to be good friends.

You heard about the storm comin'?
          He asks, never looking over

The same storm slicing
          through every inch of armor
          my binder becoming more unbearable as the sun sets.

          Yes. I knew about the storm coming.

Grey sky to match the sea
       pops against spears of orange
          yellow leaves

          some throaty musk
     like salt & clay flirting in mud
& we, well I, had never seen the water
come up this high

          lovely in its terror,
          getting darker

    full moon behind us,
          as we're absorbed into
              the damp questions
              posed by subway tunnels.

*

prince died for fem bois

I said I only want to fuck the taste out of your mouth
& I meant it as a furnace. I meant burn manhood
down in button up crop tops. I mean burn it down
H O U S E Q U A K E like angering Prince as aunty
the one with money & two separate couch sets.
The one in the front room & its flecks of floral sweats
choked in plastic. It squeezes my ass, bites my thighs
stinging nettles, but it's hers so I must comply.
She glides in on her icy boundaries, says the plastic
one is for company. Family is a kind of company.
Manhood: the dirty fingers sliding into our plotted
eternity. I'll burn every uncovered couch set for you
my prince, my aunt, my queen. When I find it I will
kill manhood with fire — it is a tick that poisons
our infinity. Purposeless, nasty & cruel. Faggotry
is the way to nurture the fire. Faggotry is also the way
to snuff the fire to steam of memory. Even
a tick has purpose — to be devoured by peacocked
majestics beating their oiled wings in miraculous flight
& we are still fucking. Still thinking of fem princeliness
coronated by queenliness. Crown placed, sword
sworn by auntie. Watching ticks pop on the match.

new york > brooklyn > casual encounters > t4m >

I fear your manishness
          as the vacuum of you sucks
          up the pinks and the yellows
the beiged out lights that frame you.

I wanted your manishness
          inside of me somehow some
          enima or laxitive
of swallowed copper pennies

but you're just some normie shit.
          In dreaming I sight your cock
          pulled behind you, cupped hands push
a river to either side.

The coffee tinged water pulse
          cracked by your swerving body
          fat with gulped copper pennies.
I wanted your manishness

inside me somehow: to bite
          your biceps apart, to eat
          through your bones, to suck your cock
or perhaps to castrate you

like me. Like me, like me I
          tell the boy from school. Hormones
          bleating to be bolted sheep.
On occasion, I trail him

to tunnels of open green
      and golden light, with no noise
      and some children. Blame the thick
oil that tears through my legs,

or the life oven in me.
      Dream boy is an evergreen
      tunnel of emerald fragments
bludgeoned to chips by black waves.

a review of *Hamilton: An American Musical*

If I could go back in time, which is a game
I am sometimes forced to play I would lynch
george washington Standing there in step
with slaves whose teeth he yanked out & wore
for oil paintings & public appearances
also auctions, to be sure My boyfriend & I
won the *Hamilton* lottery last week ($10
of course) Every beige actor singing on a wheel
O New York! O New York! GREATEST CITY!
Over a field of black bones scraped clean
The subway is also a boneyard The papers
won't tell me where so I say everywhere, except
nobody but nobodies care what I think I joined
The Organization because I wanted to practice
holding america hostage *Huckleberry Finn* stage
coach robbers 219 times the nigger That's the hardest
part of the whole thing: nobody cares what I think
Unless I frighten them Nothing ever resolves
itself in america No incentive, you see All
fireworks are just replicas of some foreign
bomb They drop bombs & bronze sculptures
for every genocide anyway Somebody says
we bouta bomb North Korea Nobody cares
what I think america is an experiment lit up
by sparking wires Oh please Oh please
let it burn down this time

doppelgänger

Queer utopians think human beings are perfectible
but we're not, we're just correctable.

In an hourly motel, I recall that Kim Addonizio poem about tattoos
& ask you how many you have, although I count fourteen
everytime you doze & add your spit to the mysterious stains on the pillows.

But the ink proliferates in twilight's sticky gold: is a cover up one or two or three tattoos?
& how many about your forced disappearances?
& how many about the appearance of manhood?
& how many about being a man
with his face buried in pillows — a short, black man hydroplaning down our impossible?

I hate how much I love
when you suck my toes & I despise you
for making me beg. That's why I can't know you, that's why I stay
perpetually ahead of your judgement. You look just like me

when I'm fucking you from behind. I'll suck that shrimp cock 'till the glove pops
plus one extra wop before I figure it out. I don't know god anymore
but let's stay here on our knees & wait for him to come.

belial & morningstar & andromalius
& baraqijal & penemuel & ronobe & zegan

Everybody knows I know a secret.
I've stared at windows until hands poked through
and I've nursed men left on my doorstep
with stern, unshorn nipples like fraying tissue.

We learned we could never go home, at least
not without making pistols of ourselves.
I was made to jaw on your fennel stalk;
we were made and raised to raise the fallen

and lift them high by their turgid taproots.
Everyone's heard I saw two king snakes fuck.
Everyone knows I know who gets more pleasure
(The pleasure arrives for the taker, who takes
cacophonously —   superfluously —)
The *YES! PLEASE!* fuck. The *no, go home* finish.

           The *YES! PLEASE!* fuck finished, so run home
           on the white bus clouded by need. Ya mama
           wonders who's been over. Says it was a black.
           She can smell it. Must have been Blue Magic

           smeared over your pillowcase. My head shape
           dented and scented and haunting your fingertips.
           Anyone but a black, she thinks.
           Someone pretty and black, my mother hopes.

                              In this scene, no one gets what they've wanted.
                                    In this scene, you Ask Jeeves "penis envy."
                                          In this scene, you fly me to Arizona
              four stained fingers twist — twist —, inside, push — push —
                                          In every mirror you find a demon
              four stained fingers twist — twist —, inside, push — push —

In this house there is no god but Downelink
in this apartment we take rent in rimming
in this hovel you flash your dick on Path Trains
in this shack I suck you deep on the pier

in this delusion you kiss me in public
in this delusion I meet your parents
in this delusion we have soft babies
in this delusion you keep a steady

job. You are hard work. You are brute labor.
You are original sin in house paint,
and the tripod upon which the Pythia sat
and words repel you and my tongue does not
and we become sentient and escape
and string back into the Gordian knot.

                              You oxcart king. You spiked silver seller
                            turned gold-stroker in the fire and tar woods
                          behind my house, framed in white flame. Antlers
                          draped in tiny lights we learned were beetles.

                                  You did it. I let you and you did it.
                                    Blood magic & Hennessy: I'm sorry.
                              I promise you — I paid, and paid, and paid
                          with eight years of no good dick, with violence.

Blood magic & Hennessy: I'm sorry.
If you must know, I loved you in loops
:first I'd puke on you, then watch you fold drawers,
little squares of black in Red Hook Houses.

Daddy. I look for you in other faces
changed by years of no good dick and violence.

In this scene, I Google "penis envy"
my stern, unshorn nipples like fraying tissue.

Daddy, I look for you in other faces
four stained fingers twist — twist —, inside, push — push —

You must know that I loved you in loops,
blood magic, and Hennessy. I'm sorry.

In this hovel, you flash your dick on Path Trains
changed by years of no goodness and violence.

In this delusion I meet your parents,
have soft babies, you keep a steady job.

Behind our house, framed in white flame: antlers
draped with tiny lights we learned were beetles.

Everyone's heard I saw two king snakes fuck.
Everybody knows I know a secret.

a machine of mahogany and bronze II

Almost empty early evening
                    train car.
                    We're looking
out the same yawned window,
                    hands always
                    nearly touching
then
        then casually as accidents.
                    His biceps and forearms
relaxing slightly, dozing off
                    so he
                    pulls them
back into his lap, or
                    in pockets
                    & even then
                    still touching me.

Water to our ankles
floods the stairs. Gold
Timberlands
soaked to a soiled
dinge cringing watch
the speckled tide rise.

Nobody on the street
                              but the wind.
Bare trees sway & crack
like soldier's bones.

We toss up
the hoods of
our jackets.

                A streetlight
                blown out.
                              Another.

                So I
                   ask if I
                   can kiss him.

*

We embraced in privacy
such was the veil of wind

The bash & slam
of branches then whole
limbs.
A dog barks
its muffled perplex
soon whimpers.

Bulldozer grumble
of the loveliest
plane tree on the block.

New swollen
alarm sound
in roaring
to final rest.

My mother filled the tub
in any storm, just in case.

A vision of my mother drowning,
mouth full of fetid water.

Blunt still a sticky lump
on my thrifted table—unlit.

Moments prior, his fingers
slick lips flit smooth
shape then stop.

Shove it in my mouth shaking,
tears frame its half lit tip

How's Ms. Rochelle? he asks,
taking the lighter from my useless fingers
as I pull hard enough to leave a dot of ash
on my still-wet jeans.

*

Work's rituals disguised as punishments
delivered with flat, open hand—late fee, tip out,
where tits could be out and when to hide
their inky points—I knelt for the hymn of each
house rule. I paid house mom her $10
and paid the DJ his $20. I paid after every dance
and as I walked through the steel door blocking
us from daylight and people who look out bright windows.
The habits of the work metered by costume changes
in head counts, in raids. You wouldn't know this
but they always pick the dry days to bust
trust desperation's needle on the bone, its chalk-smooth
breath making the needs of the skin stronger
than the desire to protect the next day.
Obvious in their baldness and their softening muscles
grabbing your ass to pull your attention away
from men whose dollars stack in neat little chimneys
for the shadow of your heat. Men near the end of hot wings.
Men looking through the foot of a pint glass. Men ready
to spend money, but for this intrusion and so many
empty seats at the bar. The girls on the shift circle
descending as he shoos another away until too few stools
are filled by the lowest sort of men, dregs of a poison well.
And they don't tip, and they never smile honestly, just sneer
barely glancing at the flesh though it sparkles and winks.
Lap dance like fisticuffs—bruises and short blood
in the folds of the body, then return a while later, but soon
enough to still wear the bloom he's sown in you.
This time I was on schedule, I had already tipped in my $40.
He paid for 30 minutes in the rooms with a door and a couch
before I could count a full song his raw throb and no question.
His arm a rope dredging the dip in my back. His face a composite
of men I'd seen before but jaw so hard you can, imagine

the last skull he broke with boot tip or bull club. Clear
the consequence, sharp the pain that I couldn't fit
in its rightful context. I dazed my eyes to the carpet
until it was over. I set my bag on the counter
at my slice of mirror, stained with the too-rich blush
I tried once but gave to a new young girl in lingerie
so she wouldn't spit on two taboos that night.
Smeared thumbprint of sable foundation
from my most recent $1000 night, when I celebrated
with both hands up and one leg on the countertop.
I ran to the doorless bathroom stall to eject
the worry that had entered me. A Long Island
with Patrón sidecar waiting for clients and cat daddies
who would pad in when they came, stiff on their legs
soft in their desire for the body, naked in their want
for warm comfort, their nasty hunger flowing over.
My all whites: dress, g-string, see through Pleasers
with the two straps. Only ingenues and pros
can milk a Sunday, hold it captive until it changes
it's name from weekend to workday, so only three
of us there. Enough to find the end of the night
as sore as we were rich if a crowd surprised us.
Russell, a regular, stopped by to drop some money,
so I told the DJ play "I'd Rather Be with You"
just him, two white guys & me up there slow grindin
with the pole, the mirror, the chaise lounge.
Then the outside light halved around all those faces
in one face talking too long and too loud
at the manager, jutting his chin at me. I don't see.
I see with my gut. I see him, snaking his arm around
others. We will all spend the night close together.
Russell ordered a shot and finished his game.

*　　*

Asar searches the answers on my face
       until a strand of lightning blows the bulbs out.

              I rush to fill the tub
              before its mouth
              drains brown.

He endeavors to start a seven day candle
       with a lighter. I don't correct him.

       Success an orb of flickering white-yellow
       light growing aware of its own existence

       by casting his shadow:
       the silhouette
       of an illuminated saint
       in fuzzy braids.

Asar could have been my high school sweetheart

    if such a term applied
    to relationships kept secret.

    He hadn't softened:
       bulbous knuckles
       forever framing
          something on fire.

    He leans in close enough to shotgun
       then exhales away, breathing into uncertain flame.

My lips hang slack and open
gloss at their rim.

I squeeze my arms tight around me, sighing my embarrassment
                    he holds my chin in the soft trap of his fingers
                            my bottom lip wrapped up in his.

The burning wick swallowed
            scorching down my throat
                        tripping over flotsam
                                as I shove open the clogged door.

Asar strips off his first layer of shirts

                    me, choking
                    noticing every new ripple
                    in his skin and sinew of copper.

            Chest piece I don't remember
            G-O-D-F-O-R-G-I-V-E-S
            I piece together through the openings
            of an A shirt
                        bleached stiff.

Candle, consort
            close enough for me to fear

            as I study him from the wobbly double bed
                        ass up and too clothed.

He joins me. Small circle of light still looking

reaching towards us
        thumb stroking the fuzz
        at the small of my back.

    Neither feigns surprise.

            Chill & ache of familiar teeth
        pull my
                    collarbone

            tailbone

            pits of knees

        licked lips brush
                crest of hip & valley
            of navel

    and whatever watches looks
    until the light is all but lost.

The sun barely rises
in its furious sky

            but what little does emerges
            from the recess between his hip

            and the half circle of his chest

    still bearing
    sweat stained
    shirt second skin.

                        *

In the night I filled his dimples with milk
brilliant thimbleful, then again, again   a sturdiness
on whose oakstead arms   I swing.

A preener for the guillotine   the brush & comb & droplet & spritz pulled
forever over the swoop of his edges
in anticipation of every potential open casket

gaping for even small defiances.   I've spent dream-days
          sipping cream from his melting jawline
licking the grave dust from hooves of suede and steel toe.

I'm prepared to tear one-thousand additional mornings   body angled over
          treacherously inadequate cushions   sucking saltwater
lazing forth from his diligent navel.

Atlantic be damned.   Sluice your volume
through every of our new-broken windows   pierce
as we do—with sin, with everyday, with a wholeness.

My ouroboros & rupture   my undoing onto death's
          custard pus   make of me your swept bloat, sunlight burst
marrow fruit. Steep me in your murderous light   here, in this bed
growl no threat   arrive with the stun of your knife.

*

If you must be raped, may all your rapes
be short rapes. May there be some pleasant
sound or thought in the frozen cell you keep
inside yourself for retreat in such dire conditions.
When you are prostrate to the reality of your body
may you sleep awake until he is finished, until
you smell him step beyond the door frame
and hear the click of the door settling back
into the blameless jamb: the lock, its key, its gear,
the wheel of your life losing momentum
and settling, finally, into its groove. May you retain
your sense of privacy. May you regain privacy quickly.
May you remember quiet. Quiet. Silent. No crashing
to never digest, to always remember. No, for you
softer even than a cat's ear. For you, the clay taste
—rain through the window, the drip of the rain,
the distraction of some other part of the body
adding its key to the slow, low-wailing drag.
May you seek refuge in coming apart under
the pressure of the body like too-chewed gum.
May every fragment locate its escape route.
May it slip with a yawn at the tear of his hook.
May you glide along the blade of the truth: nothing
could take as long, or as much, as this took.

*   *

"MATURE BUCKS WALK INTO THE WIND WHENEVER POSSIBLE"
(and are well suited to blue-violet and yellow)

sun stiff line whose boundaries, constricted by dusk buck. landscape: gnawed open gates and flashlights startle to jumping point. one shits down its hind legs which doesn't impede the men edging nearer open left hand, right curdled over shocker's hilt. perhaps if we were all just still, just quiet, but drummed murmur metal box crunching us up its sides zooming where until at last we arrive at the life dump. sinister land of no-more. licked the fences until uncertain yoke broke the pink bumps. tawny chain gang singing birdshot *if I could just if I could just* and feel waves rush. the train came, you know, after the bell. but if I could just, I could just get. this. spike. out my back before the door yawns, before the fingered things send lightning, I'd run home, barely beyond the bullet.

an eight year old with asperger's contemplates suicide

the blue whale at the museum's lonely
missing all her titan kin
face of plaster, veins of tin
she bellows her trauma in effigy

when I was a child on the lip of the woods
preachers lectured on Jonah's hubris
and I'd think I don't need to know this
I just wanted to live in the sea. no good

was religion, I'd set my inner vision
on the brooks and the rivers
that drained in the sea — a giver
who held us imprisoned, but diluted their poisons

with conch shells and salt memory. in play-doh and felt
I'd sculpt blue whale and narwhal so deeply I felt
I belonged to the sea.

chewbacca was the blackest part of *The Force Awakens*

Black excitement is danger. We have seen the other side of optimism for so long.
Feels like fiction. Put your feet up on that dashboard because here comes
the F U T U R E! Wow! Chewbacca was the blackest part of *The Force Awakens*.
Fucked Kylo Ren's shit up over his nigga Solo. Millennium Falcon with that white boy
so *Homeboys in Outer Space*. When we colonize the stars, everyone will be beige,
white folks sometimes say, or orange. White people in Chalmette are orange
& I'll never forget it. 2050 or 2040 or 2020. Chewbacca was the blackest part of *The Force
Awakens*. Always moaning & never understood. Always hunted & never going home.

Fin could barely hold a lightsaber or even a gun. Always inept & always ready
to run. Lando Calrissian. Gambling or picking up trash. Whatever. Steal a black
man's ride. Look! Steals leather jacket. Drapetomania & Rascality & you can't
trust that coon. Chewbacca was the blackest part of *The Force Awakens*,
because black danger is excitement. Pickaninnies escape the busy jaws
of the tiger only sometimes and are sometimes chomped through by each crocodile,
or tasered by droids, or pummeled by batons for no reason at all. Or snuffed
like poisoned roaches at the local AME Church or shot down in the street
and left to rot in the high red sun like crushed possum. Raccoon.
And I am just too tired. Too vengeful to go anywhere anymore.

YES! it was I who sucked extras out of your holes!

DAT ASSSSSS! Exclaimed my manager as I teetered
off stage each Sunday, three song set sweatily ended
— an auction packed with feckless, hard-dicked breeders
palming their cocks through their pants, tongues extended
and grabbing my, then, Apollonian biceps, my family-feeders.
I dangled from a trinity of vertical rails, artfully suspended
and showed runaway girls my tricks so they wouldn't need the stroll
cause they could get that money up on the pole.

Slow day desperation and hunger at the month's nadir
I count the number of dudes who may want some head
like a neon lion in a slingshot and clear heels sniffs bloodless air,
hoping I didn't fuck up and pick a cop who would steal my bread.
(Didn't want to end the night locked up or dead.)
A white guy, with two grown sons in hockey jerseys, appears;
his glass of warm beer glows in blacklight as if hewn from lead,
and cries out *DAT ASSSSSS!* as I dance for the mirror.
I slip into their party, inform each of my price;
the dad calls me a nigger, slides $200, says it twice.

You said you've been to the club, but I don't believe you

since you do not remember the phosphorescent sweat
        or the nausea of midday neon lights, their translucent venom.
                Anything can be amusing if it isn't happening to you. In public

I am forgetful, the margin of my shifts melt butter-slick
        the milky way is just another fluorescent bulb, screaming needless
                wattage. Jesus, somebody throw the goddamn switch

but I'll never forget the way ink-embossed Baby Phat cat crept
        through the desert of your lower back, your fetish for makeshift spinal taps
                your fuck machine. Your name reminded you and only you of Egypt,

Dynasty showed you how to flip without kicking; she's worked
        underground for two years and wants an eighteenth birthday
                party in the champagne room. When cops shredded your asshole

you was just a baby; you're grown now. You cried the first time a customer
        finger-fucked you while you wasn't looking. Lexus said *watch better*
                next time. You watch good — so good, you sip gin with Red Bull in it
                you stalk the night.

a machine of mahogany and bronze III

There are trunks full of people like me.
        There are dumpsters full of women late for shifts
                but no one knows if they have the name to ask after

let alone on her house phone
        these barrel, car, train   track women.
                Why call to ask for a name her mother didn't know?

There are miles of club parking lots with coworkers
        dismantled   hushed by packed snow
            behind after hours spots that charged her
        for missing her stage call. The obvious choices

are first lost, their names whispered behind them
        both eulogy and physical description: Tiny. Lil' Bit.
            The girls disappeared by a shadow named

to revise an old opinion or highlight a trait
        to let you know what you're getting: Envy. Vixen. Treasure.
            The hometown names tasted at the base of their tongues

or imaginations. Brooklyn. Philly. L.A. Luxurious things carried off
        behind silent headlights: Diamond. Lexxis. Mercedes.
            But never the solid names, the regal ones
mid-earners with thoroughbred legs. Until sweet Legacy
        with an ass like mine, taller than me in her little four inch heels.

*   *

The train's running on time again. The general
        assembly meeting planned minutes ago
        is scheduled for five. I preempt the conquest
attempted by roomates returned from elsewhere
to their own bathroom and ready to stay a while,
        drained the tub
and through the solid
        hover of steam
        I saw a newly opened toothbrush
        facedown in
its wrapper, flecks
        of paste all over
        I rinsed it off and later
        set it on my windowsill
to dry feeling not like lovers
        but cutting close.

        I would walk
        the ten blocks to his house
        late night when
Terrence came home drunk
        the sound of my mother screaming at my back
        plaster walls smashed
by the weight of her body

& fall asleep tangled
        on the felt blankets arranged
        beside his bed frame

& before dawn he would
        unfold his sheets
        for me to climb inside   radiate
        warmth & safety
        until morning.

I'd come home to blood
                crushed into the carpet
& my mother, drunk
                passed out on the couch:
                now hopelessly
stained. I always hoped this
                would mean he, too,
                was asleep, too placid to wake to my
                footsteps, but

His was an energetic, wrathful

                sort of drunkenness

and there was enough

                to go around. Violence

enough for all those

                in the vicinity of his rage

*

In my still dark and silent a radio
hisses up my neck. Nothing new
or novel, just the reality of water
not quite news because I could've
briefed the forecaster   the geyser
blowing. Drip. Trickle. Hose. Stream.
The black wild   surrounds the lot.

I do well to decipher the mumbles
of nearby men. They are leaving.
Their wives are worried. They say
they cannot swim. They say *leave if you want*
forehead lines lie serious and foolish.
They have packed coolers full of bread
and milk. The walls are all drip and bloat.
They melt into soup each hour until nothing.

*   *

It's a full week since
          the last Decolonize
          check-in. Awkward
gathered here again.

For months message
          threads lit up dawn, dusk
          late nights, desperate for
one another ground

muddy, unsteady
          below us, coming for us
          sucking tides. Alisha's
court date set, next

Monday. Apparently
          the collective already
          flyered to pack the court
Jamila made an event

three days ago, said
          she had added me as an
          admin. Kwame called, left
a message. What else

could I have thought
          of but my mother, drowning
          heavy debt I thought
she should tender.

Believing in my own
          owedness. Apology from time
          someone else's action she
watched in fear

for letting him shove me
          out the door to hurt her in
          private. For his drunken
specter shouting bile

for hours until I tired.

A mother certain
          I shared the blame
          for his anger. Who insisted
he was forgivable

Now my mother
          anonymous, drowning. Scowling
          I tell this to the caucus, the fact
of flooding. No one

yet sure of how much
          or how many. Why not focus
          our energies here? I have never
seen my mother swim

and feel sick with
          uncertainty. We could go staggered
          separate busses, protest at the gate
write letters, blocades

obstruct funders
       businesses. *Or you could go find*
       your mother Jamilah intruded
as people who know nothing intrude.

I was swept through
       with bitter and salt, couldn't
       catch my breath sobbing
snot dripping pushed away
with the side of my palms.

*

Break with me the steel of the trunk, bulleted throughout
concealed by a layer of thin carpet that knucks as the kick
of a horse drums and peels skin from whatever follows.
The meat white and small as chicklet teeth. The borders
crumbling in the droning hum. Radiant clatter at the boundary
of your life. Yes. You. Here with me now in the isolation. Break
with me and flood the irons. Clutch the closing note of a field
holler intercepted by the branding iron. The mutter rushes
its intention to rupture. Clear as the alarms. Horns.
Speaker. Gutter sounds from any mouth around me.

Other pods of women knitted
one the other with knotted pant
legs, lengths of pipe, bits of wire.
Many more float, bloated in the
coursing water: putrid & somber.
Heads now only a few inches
below the cracking roof shining
open patches of daylight. Sludge.
A queer absence of birds & signs

Someone once a someone leans into arm,
shoulder, claws the base of my head.
A corpse of empathetic boyance. Vague
prediction is still prophecy in the muse's mouth.

Dust & pebbles coat the surface
We cup our hands beneath each
other's armpits rearing back, a clean
hit. Vicious suck crunch through roof
not our doing. Cement boulders dive
from above leaving jagged holes
pellet rain. Survivors scatter pushed
below the everlast. No one to know.

Still small babies, loved
by grandmother, aunty beset
with curiosity but never a body
recognizable enough to bury.

No one scanning sea lights
for bobbing suspended empties
drifting out smashed windows
becoming full moon Atlantic. Lost
concern in the single, ancient silence.

*   *

Asar's rusted Crown Victoria
  stuttering through each stoplight
  river to the right, too
high, a few small

branches down & street
  lights cracked or bent
  highway lanes drained
but swept with silt.

New York can't stand
  the insult of hurricane wind
  but more words gurgle from the split.
We slip time

hollering then silent
  back into the archaic
  lap and fold of the ocean.
Shit. It's not about what I believe

but I believe black folks
  got gills secreted away
  in our necks, ever ready
to become post

terrestrial. Asar
  tired from ten hour shift
  now it's near 1 AM but I
just need to see.

His wire driving
        glasses glare as we jerk
        at the caution sign a quarter
mile away

with a sigh drawn out.
        We turned back towards
        home. What had I expected
to see? What could

be learned after
        midnight on a flooded road? Jittered
belly feels vomit

coming. I clamor
        from the deep velour
        seats, out onto the shoulder
propelled by sadness

steadied by
        the indestructible
        car door. Residual
mud puddles

squished into
        the holes in the soles
        of my black leather boots
rain speckling

soft enough
        to disregard now, dying
        shortly. Out of breath

once distant

     waves splashed over the

     length of the washed out

road, suspended

in still hungry water.

.

*

It's not so difficult to die this way   lungs pulling until swole with blank   fluid. It will take years, but soon
I will be a liquid. First, snow. Push   my way to the bottom of everything.   One gap maw preceding bristle
teeth. Baleen can't help but admit   what's left of my body. Yes, the sea   is cluttered with wide noses,
with royal gaps.   There is nothing special   about the ending except being
received by godly fingers, & thrust   of small beads & shells   as the light collapses.

This, my everlasting mattress of silt

    A life of pressed dissent in an era of decline.

        There's a silk to the glide through the cracks

of a botched house. There's a clap to the door

    and a snap to the teeth of its lock. Salt-like

        lapping up whatever wasn't wiped away.

Forever a convenient disappearance. Anyway,

    mine is an acre of submerged acres, a queer mirror

        of where I was born: where height becomes depth

air is abundant, but secreted in fissures

    released in a flutter as if gathered pearls, solid as dry masts.

        Now and then, a streak of alien light on a beam

of sound cuts the solemnity of the blackening
water some religious and singular wonder.

Acknowledgments

Thank you to *make/shift magazine*, *The Wanderer*, *WUSSY*, *femmescapes*, and *Nat. Brut* where "jersey fem/mes in the philly zoo", "prince died for fem bois", " "yes! it was I who sucked extras out of your holes!", "an elegy for the family (w)rex", "my stepfather mouthfucks the devil", and "MATURE BUCKS…" appeared in earlier forms.

Many thanks to my most influential teachers: Susana Loza, Monica Youn, Camile Rankine, aracelis girmay, Sharon Bridgforth, Margo Jefferson, Dorothea Lasky, Timothy Donnelly, Jay Deshpande, Lee Siegel, Hilton Als, L'Mani Viney, and Christopher Tinson.

Thank you to the places whose support helped make this work: Culture/Strike, Leeway Foundation, Astraea Foundation, Rewire News/Disabled Writers, Columbia University, and the Davis-Putter Scholarship Fund.

Thank you to my friends J.D. Stokely, Petra Floyd, Najee Haynes-Follins, Riley Ramanathan, and Leah Lakshmi Piepzna-Samarasinha for being sweetly challenging collaborators, thought artists, and early readers of this work.

Thank you to my family. Thank you to Azure D. Osborne-Lee. And a final deep and secret thanks to NLN.

Cyrée Jarelle Johnson is a writer and librarian living in New York City. They are a candidate for an MFA in Creative Writing at Columbia University. In 2018 their work appeared in *The New York Times*, *Boston Review*, *Rewire News*, *The Root*, *Nat. Brut*, and *WUSSY*. They have given speeches, lectures, and spoken on panels at The White House, The Whitney Museum of American Art, The University of Pennsylvania, The Philadelphia Trans Health Conference, Tufts University, and Mother Bethel AME Church, among other venues. Their work has been profiled on PBS Newshour and Mashable. Cyrée Jarelle has received fellowships and grants from Culture/Strike, Leeway Foundation, Astraea Foundation, Rewire News/Disabled Writers, Columbia University, and the Davis-Putter Scholarship Fund. They are a founding member of The Harriet Tubman Collective and The Deaf Poets Society.

Nightboat Books

Nightboat Books, a nonprofit organization, seeks to develop audiences for writers whose work resists convention and transcends boundaries. We publish books rich with poignancy, intelligence, and risk. Please visit nightboat.org to learn about our titles and how you can support our future publications.

The following individuals have supported the publication of this book. We thank them for their generosity and commitment to the mission of Nightboat Books:

Kazim Ali

Anonymous

Jean C. Ballantyne

Photios Giovanis

Amanda Greenberger

Anne Marie Macari

Elizabeth Motika

Benjamin Taylor

Jerrie Whitfield & Richard Motika